Genoa
Travel Guide

Quick Trip

D1440489

Table of Contents

BUDGET TIPS 43

KNOW BEFORE YOU GO 61

Genoa

With its lovely setting between the Italian Riviera coast

and the mountains, Genoa is fast becoming an alternative

holiday destination to Italian cities like Florence and

Rome. Genoa has is an interesting historical city centre

with a number of cultural attractions and is a good choice

for an active outdoors or sporting holiday.

GENOA TRAVEL GUIDE

The surrounding mountains offer good hiking with trails like the Alta Via dei Monti Liguri winding their way through thick forests punctuated by waterfalls and lakes. Little villages along the way are a welcome respite from the summer heat and great places to stop for a bite to eat. Down at sea level the beaches stretch for miles and a variety of watersports are on offer as well as fishing and sailing all of which are great ways to spend a day.

Viewed from a distance the city of Genoa rambles up the wooded slopes of the Apennine Mountains, with the houses and buildings painted in mostly warming shades making splashes of orange, red and pink amongst the dark green.

Genoa has the largest medieval city centre in Europe and owes much of its success to the Middle Ages when it was

GENOA TRAVEL GUIDE

a thriving and busy port. Unlike some maritime cities Genoa is still very much a working port, not just for sailing boats and cruise liners but it is also a very busy shipping port with ship building and breaking yards.

The best place to find all the action is on the waterfront and in the area of Porto Antico. Redesigned in 1992 by Renzo Piano for the Columbus Celebration the port is now the heart of all cultural events, shows, exhibitions and entertainment in Genoa.

Tourists and locals enjoy gentle strolls along the harbour and through the nearby 12th century Via Sottoripa. Here under the porticoes brightly coloured shops sell dried fruits and delicious smelling spices while tempting aromas waft out of the restaurant doors.

GENOA TRAVEL GUIDE

For families the Città del Bambini in Porto Antico is a super play centre for children and close by there is the Bigo lift, an ice rink and a multi-cinema. Naturally there are plenty of places for refreshments and retail therapy with bars, cafés and restaurants and a choice of shops.

The largest aquarium in Europe can be found in the port area as well as the Museum of the Sea. Many visitors purchase the combined Acquario Village ticket which gives discounts on the mini-train linking the attractions as well as on admission prices.

In the city you can wander along the atmospheric alleyways surrounded by a sense of history before emerging into piazzas filled with light and noise. The main square is Plaza de Ferrari where the Palaces of the

GENOA TRAVEL GUIDE

Doges can be found close to the chic shopping area of Via XX Settembre.

There are cobbled passageways which can be quite narrow but worth the effort as they lead you to ancient churches or streets where quaint bars and boutiques await you. At the opposite end of the scale the wide and impressive Via Garibaldi is lined with Renaissance palaces decorated by local and foreign artists and built to house important Genoan families.

For a relaxing swim and some sunbathing you can hop on a bus or train to the nearby beaches of which Nervi, Quinto and Quarto are the best ones. A short boat ride will take you to San Fruttoso with its rather interesting underwater statue and picturesque Abbey. Walking along the red brick path which follows the coastline is how many people who visit this part of Italy spend their time. Along the way there are charming fishing villages, cosy restaurants and ice-cream shops.

From the viewpoint at Castelletto you can admire the widespread views across the city to the mountains beyond and for any taphophiles or tombstone tourists the Cemetery of Staglieno is a fascinating place to visit with extravagant chapels and hundreds of statues.

The cuisine in the region is excellent; being a port city naturally there is a lot of seafood and fish on the menu. Local specialities are of course pesto, focaccia, farinata, breasola, gnossci and bruschetta. Eating out in Genoa is still relatively cheap compared to many Italian cities as long as you don't mind eating with the locals in some of the less fancy restaurants.

Opportunities for smart dining though abound in Genoa and where better to go than to Zeffirino's where Frank Sinatra once visited to eat Italian pesto. Don't miss the chance to try Pesto alla Genovese. This local green delight made from fresh basil and pine nuts is served with French beans and slices of potato missed in with trofie pasta.

🌏 Customs & Culture

As the European capital of Culture and Art in 2004 it goes without saying that Genoa has much to offer visitors looking to explore more than just the Old Port and surrounding countryside. This is the city with the biggest cultural centre in Europe and the streets of the Old Town of Genoa are listed as a UNESCO World Heritage Site and have a unique Ligurian atmosphere.

GENOA TRAVEL GUIDE

There is an excellent selection of art galleries and museums representing different styles and periods throughout history. This is a city that has been given the nickname of *la Superba* or the Proud One because of its impressive landmarks and glorious past.

One of the largest yearly events in Genoa is the International Boat Show which has been held every October since 1962. Everything nautical is on display along with 400 boats and some 50 super yachts.

Another maritime event is the historic regatta which is held the first weekend in June between teams of eight rowers in gaily decorated boats. The festival is a competition between the cities of Amalfi, Pisa, Venezia

GENOA TRAVEL GUIDE

and Genoa and rotates between them; thus being held every four years in Genoa.

At the end of July the Gezmataz Festival draws music lovers to the Arena del Mare. This is Genoa's piazza by the sea where concerts are held and the crowds enjoy balmy evenings and the strong and lively beat of jazz under the night-time skies. Another festival in July is the Goa Boa rock and hip hop festival and then in August the Festival Musicale del Mediterraneo brings shows and concerts together from different parts of the world.

Other events throughout the year include the traditional celebrations of Holy Week when the most spectacular one to watch has to be the evening procession on Holy Thursday. There are also poetry festivals, science events, theatre events and in December the centre of this historic city is taken over by the Festival of Clowns.

🌍 Geography

The Italian city of Genoa is sandwiched between the Apennine Mountains and the Ligurian Sea at the top of this boot-shaped country and is around 160km from the French border. The setting of Genoa couldn't be much better and the 600,000 inhabitants spend a lot of time outdoors in the fresh air, walking or taking part in watersports or just soaking up the sun on the beaches.

The city is part of the triangle of industrial cities of Milan-Turin-Genoa in the north-west and plays a major part in the economics of the country. It is the largest port in Italy and since the 19th century vast steelworks and shipyards have been part of the skyline. Believed to be the first of its kind in the world the Bank of Saint George was founded here in 1407 making it one of the oldest financial institutions in the world.

Genoa is excellent transportation-wise especially by train. It is a main hub for many routes and connects with the Italian cities of Turin, Milan, Rome, La Spieza and Pisa and also Nice in France. There are two train stations in central Genoa; Brignole and Principe so check you are going to the right one for the train you want to catch. Brignole is generally for more local routes and has some bus connections as well.

The buses leave from Piazza della Vittoria for destinations in many European countries. The Euroline coach company is the main operator using fast, clean and comfortable coaches to whisk you across Europe.

The small city airport of Cristoforo Colombo has daily flights to other destinations in Italy and across Europe and there is a shuttle bus between the airport and the city centre.

From the port it is possible to catch a ferry to Elba, Sardinia, Corsica and Sicily. There is also a weekly ferry to Barcelona and the trip on the Grand Navi Veloci takes about 18 hours. If a boat trip to Tangiers grabs your attention it will take rather longer at 46 hours.

Weather & Best Time to Visit

The climate in Genoa is classified as borderline Mediterranean and humid sub-tropical as only one month in the summer sees less than 40mm of rainfall. It is also a very windy city. There are over 2000 hours of sunshine per year with an average of four per day in the winter rising to nine in the summer.

The springtime brings a feeling of rebirth to the city after the gloomy winter months as the gardens and parks burst into life. This time of year is the peak of the basil growing season in Liguria and the fragrant scent fills the streets. The temperatures rise steadily from 8°C to 20°C and jumpers and jackets can be left at home when taking a walk in the park.

Family days out can begin and there is nowhere better in the city to take a spring picnic than Parc Avventura. By the end of May the sea is warm enough to swim in but the beaches are still quiet as summer tourists are yet to arrive.

GENOA TRAVEL GUIDE

The summer months are naturally the warmest as to be expected in this region and the temperatures range between 17°C and 28°C. Long sunny days can be spent sightseeing or lazing on the beaches and strolling along promenades in the warm evenings. Dining al fresco is a pleasure as the heat of the day has gone leaving behind comfortable temperatures.

Autumn in Genoa can be lovely; particularly the earlier part of the season as the cooler weather doesn't arrive until November time due to the shelter of the mountains. The weather is still pleasant enough for sightseeing but the winter chills have yet to set in and the temperature ranges between 9°C and 24°C. The only real downside to the autumn weather is that this is the time of year when the rainfall is the heaviest.

GENOA TRAVEL GUIDE

Winter can bring snow, although it rarely settles in the city, and chilly northern winds blowing in from the Po Valley mean that a winter coat is part of the everyday wardrobe. Visitors are going to find that the winters in Genoa are relatively sunny and dry but naturally at times there will cloudy periods and a definite nip in the air. Temperatures fall to around 5°C but the high of 12°C is still much better than some countries experience in these months.

Sights & Activities: What to See & Do

🌐 Palazzo Reale

Via Balbi, 10

16126 Genoa

Tel: +39 010 2710236

From the outside the soft pinks and reds of the

symmetrical building are interspersed with golden arches.

There are small ponds and immaculately manicured

gardens with hundreds of tiny windows catching the sunlight. Inside there is only a small selection of rooms to open to the public but nonetheless it is definitely worth the effort.

The beautiful 17th century palace was built for the Balbi family and still contains much of their original furniture and fittings. A visit here is rather like stepping back in time as you pass through the ballroom and plush throne room and see the furnishings and fabrics of the family who left so long ago. The sparkling reflections of the chandeliers in the hall of mirrors are quite breathtaking and a highlight of the visit.

There are many paintings, mostly by unknown artists but a few can be seen by Van Dyck and Tintoretto. Famous or not the artwork is very good and English descriptions in each room make understanding the works easier.

The opening hours are Tuesday and Wednesday from 9am to 1.30pm and Thursday to Sunday from 9am to 7pm. The admission price is just €4 for adults and €2 for children.

🌐 Porta Soprana & Columbus House

Via di Porta Soprana,

16123 Genoa

Tel: +39 010 2516714

The two towers of the old city gates stand tall above the remains of the city wall, close to the ruins of St. Andrew's cloister and the house that is the reputed birthplace of Christopher Columbus.

Many Italian cities have walls surrounded them but Genoa has far more than any other. The first city walls built here were in the 9th century and bits were added on right up until the 17th century. The Puerta Serrana walls are a combination of construction from the 9th and 12th centuries.

A climb up the ancient staircase in one of the towers to the lookout point rewards you with some amazing views across the city as well as being excellent exercise. The towers are impressive but the location in Genoa is what makes this attraction even more special

GENOA TRAVEL GUIDE

Porta Soprana is an important reference point as it is the gateway to many of the exciting and interesting areas of the town. A little exploration in the surrounding area will find you in little streets that rarely see tourists and lined with much cheaper bars and restaurants than in the more popular places.

Columbus House is through the arch to the east and is set in a pretty little garden surrounded by dainty marble pillars. There is a small museum inside but it only takes few minutes to look round. Looking at the outside of the walls and house is free but for around €7 a combination ticket gives you access to the inside of Christopher Columbus house and the staircase of the Puerta Serrana Tower.

 San Lorenzo Cathedral

Piazza San Lorenzo

16123 Genoa

Tel: +39 010 265786

www.genova.chiesacattolica.it/

The Gothic design San Lorenzo Cathedral is the seat of the Archbishop of Genoa and its origins date back to the 5th or 6th century. Many additions and alterations have been done and the construction of the cathedral was finally finished in the 17th century. Much of the money for these reformations came from the Crusades leaving a legacy of chapels and altars for us to see with interior colonnades, beautiful frescoes and other artworks.

The unusual black and white striped façade with the three arches gives no clue as to the elaborate architecture inside. The dome inside is magnificent but under your feet the rather striking floor immediately grabs your attention as well, lit by the sun coming in the colourful stained glass windows.

Underneath the cathedral the Museum of the Treasury has a collection of beautiful pieces of silverware and jewellery from 9AD to the present day. One of the most important items on display is the chalice believed to have been used by Christ during the Last Supper.

Various excavations under the nearby pavements have discovered pre-Christian sarcophagi as well as Roman walls and other structures. The sarcophagi lead experts to believe that a burial ground exists on the site.

The opening hours are 8am until noon and 3pm until 7pm and entry is free.

La Lantana Lighthouse & Museum

Via Rampa della Lanterna,

16126 Genoa

Tel: +39 010 910001

La Lantana is the oldest lighthouse in the world that still functions. A warning system for ships was constructed on the headland around the middle of the 10th century and the current tower was first lit in 1543. Ever since then fires and lights have kept thousands of ships safely off the rocky shores of Genoa.

GENOA TRAVEL GUIDE

Today standing at a lofty 117 metres above sea level the lamp can be seen from a distance of 36 nautical miles away across the sea. Originally wood was used to fire a signal to warn the ships off the rocks but eventually oil lamps and then electricity replaced these and now the light is automated. Every 20 seconds a white light flashes twice with a 5 second gap.

Inside the lighthouse there is a museum which tells visitors through pictures and videos about the history of Genoa and its people. Legend had it that the architect responsible for designing the lighthouse was invited to the opening ceremony and then pushed off the top. He had apparently mentioned building a taller tower elsewhere and the Genoan people didn't want to be in second place.

The promenade that leads to La Lantana is open every day from 8am until sunset and the lighthouse and museum are open weekends and holidays from 10am to 6pm and 7pm in the summer. A visit to the museum and to the top of the lighthouse costs €6 with reductions for concessions.

🌐 Genoa Aquarium

Ponte Spinola

16128 Genova

Tel: +39 01023451

http://www.acquariodigenova.it/

Genoa is justifiably proud of the aquarium; it is renowned throughout Italy and is the largest in Europe and receives over a million visitors every year. The 70 tanks contain a colourful collection of ocean life from the Ligurian Sea,

Caribbean reefs and North Atlantic.

It is a fascinating place to visit with well-thought out

displays and features about bio-diversity and endangered

species. Children will love to see the dolphins diving

happily in their pool and get the chance to touch a fish

and see some very close-up sharks.

There is a small forest within the aquarium for which there

is an extra charge unless you have purchased the

combined ticket.

Here the hummingbirds fly freely around and it is

wonderful to watch them dart in and out of the trees.

There is also the neighbouring Biosfera where there are

reptiles, amphibians, insects and birds, including a very

friendly parrot, set in a mock jungle with a warm and damp climate.

For information on opening times and ticket price the website has excellent information in English as well as Italian. There are ticket combinations offering good discounts if you want to visit several attractions within the area.

🌐 Savona & Priamar Fortress

Corso Giuseppe Mazzini

17100 Savona

Tel: +39 019 822708

www.museoarcheosavona.it/

Take a trip away from the city and follow the coast road towards the French border and find the ancient Priamar

GENOA TRAVEL GUIDE

Fortress. Standing proudly on a hill overlooking the town of Savona, the fortress was built in 1542 and in medieval times was the centre of Savona. Relics and artefacts from Pre-Roman, Roman and Byzantium times have been unearthed and are now on display in the town's Archaeological Museum.

Up until a little over a century ago the fortress was used as the main military prison in Italy and was home to up to 500 prisoners. After the prison guards had left and the steel doors clanged shut for the last time the fortress was left to fall into rack and ruin. The Municipality of Savona put into operation several restoration and renewal projects and now the Priamar Fortress has a new lease of life as a multi-purpose events and cultural centre.

GENOA TRAVEL GUIDE

Within the remodeled fortress visitors can find several museums; the Purser's Palace has shows, exhibitions and performances and Sibilla's Palace where state of the art facilities are available for conferences. Every year in Donjon Square an open-air theatre stages many different and interesting productions.

You can wander round the fortress and the grounds free of charge but there is a small entrance fee for the museums. Opening hours for the Priamar Fortress Archaeological museum are mid-September to mid-June Wednesday to Friday 9.30am to 12.30pm and 2.30pm to 4.30pm. Saturday and Monday 10.30 to 3pm, closed Tuesdays. From mid-June until mid-September the hours are Monday to Saturday 10.30am to 3pm, closed Tuesday.

🌍 Musei di Strada Nuova & Palazzo Rosso, Palazzo Bianco & Palazzo Tursi

Via Garibaldi

16124 Genova

Tel: +39 010 5572193

www.museidigenova.it/

These three palaces are located near to each other in Via Garibaldi. Built as private homes for the gentry of Genoa they are now owned by the city and used as public art galleries. Inside works can be seen by such famous artists as Reubens, Caravaggio, Mattia Preti, Van Dyck, Gregorio De Ferrari, Albrecht Dürer and Guido Reni.

Via Garibaldi is a narrow paved street and it is hard to believe that it hides such wondrous buildings and museums. Make sure to look above ground level as you wind your way through the streets of Genoa as the overhead architecture can be quite striking.

In Palazzo Tursi there is less art to see but there are varied collections of tapestry, violins, coins and ceramics. Inside the Sala Paganiniana there is a small but interesting collection of artefacts and personal effects belonging to the legendary violinist Niccolò Paganini. The most treasured and revered object is his Canone violin which dates back to 1743.

Palazzo Tursi is also home to the town hall of Genoa and has been so since 1848. The opening hours for this palace are 10am to 6pm every day.

GENOA TRAVEL GUIDE

Palazzo Rosso was built between 1671 and 1877 and was owned by the Brignole Sale family until it was bequeathed by the duchess to the city. There is more than just art to see inside this elegant palace as there is some very interesting period furniture still in situ, a textile collection and cartographic and topographic collections. In Palazzo Rosso you can take the lift up to the roof and then climb the last few stairs for super 360° views of the city, especially at night.

Palazzo Bianco was built by Luca Grimaldi between 1530 and 1540 and belonged to one of the highest Genoan families. Palazzo Bianco has excellent art collections through the generosity of the Duchess of Gallilera as she donated not only her palace but her fine art collection to the city in 1884. The paintings are mainly European and from the 13th to 18th centuries.

If you are feeling peckish while visiting the palaces there is an excellent café in Palazzo Rosso. A combined ticket for entry to all three venues costing €8 can be purchased from a little bookshop between the Tursi and Bianco palaces. Some guided walking tours of Genoa also include a tour of one or more of the palaces.

Palazzos Bianco and Rosso are open Tuesday to Thursday from 9am to 7pm, Friday 9am to 11pm and Saturday and Sunday from 10am to 7pm.

See the Ligurian Mountains by Narrow Gauge Railway (Genoa to Casella)

Piazza Manin

16137 Genoa

GENOA TRAVEL GUIDE

Tel: +39 800 085311

www.ferroviagenovacasella.it/

This is a wonderful way to get away into the Ligurian countryside and see some magnificent scenery. The noisy train winds its way along 25 kilometres mainly through thick forests passing a 13th century Roman Aqueduct and the 250 acres of the Staglieno cemetery.

The train is a functioning service not a tourist train and while the carriages are not much to look at and the wheels make horrendous screeching noises the panoramic views are definitely worth it. The train schedule is a bit erratic but for something like €5 for a return ticket you can afford to wait round the station and have a coffee or two if you have just missed the train.

GENOA TRAVEL GUIDE

There are various stops along the way before reaching the final town of Casella. There is the Genoa fortress at Campi to hike up to to try some artisanal salami hop off at San Olcese Chiesa. If you fancy taking a pleasant walk along the Ciaè botanic trail hop off at San Olcese Tullo. The trail was created by the local firefighters in 1984 and there are around 32 species of flora and fauna to be seen along the way. The once deserted hamlet of Ciaè has been restored and is now a luxurious holiday chalet.

The town of Casella does not have a great deal to offer tourists and the main purpose of the journey is the train ride and the chance to see the impressive views. There is a pleasant outdoor lido to be enjoyed a short walk from the village where adults can enjoy the views the while the children splash around. Just be warned that the few shops and restaurants in Casella do still tend to have a siesta so if you arrive mid-afternoon there might not be much open.

 Albertis Castle

Corso Dogali, 18,

16136 Genoa

Tel: +39 010 272 3820

www.museidigenova.it/

Captain D'Albertis was an intrepid sea-going adventurer, writer, explorer and collector. His late 19th century home is a great tribute to his rather weird eccentricity and this is reflected in the way you access the museum. You have to take the Ascensore Montegalletto, the public lift from Via Balbi which first of all runs horizontally and then vertically.

GENOA TRAVEL GUIDE

Inside the castle you can find mementoes of the captain's voyages with trophies and frescoes decorating the rooms and the statues of Christopher Columbus show how he admired the great man. In the 'La cabina del Capitano' this tiny room is fitted out like a ships cabin and it is easy to imagine D'Albertis looking out to sea and getting lost in his fantasy world of sailing.

In the more modern section of the castle the Museum of World Cultures contains some excellent artefacts from pre-Columbian times and Native American objects.

Albertis Castle is open from 22nd March until 11th September, Tuesday, Wednesday and Friday 10am to 6pm, Thursday 1pm to 10pm and weekends 10am to 7pm. Closed on Monday. Admission prices are €6 for adults and €4.50 for concessions.

🌐 Natural History Museum of Giacomo Doria

Via Brigata Liguria, 9,

16121 Genoa

Tel: +39 010 585753

Giacomo Doria was a famous naturalist and is only fitting that in the museum that carries his name there are over forty million specimens. Doria founded the museum in 1867 and for forty years was the director of the museum.

There are paleontological collections as well as botanical, zoological, and mineralogical. The vast building was built in 1912 with two floors dedicated to public exhibitions. The 24 rooms house some six thousand animals and thousands of minerals. The rather imposing skeleton of the *elephas antiquus italicus* or straight tusked elephant graces one of the halls and is one of the highlights of the collection.

The museum is a bit outdated and there are long corridors leading to rooms with cases of stuffed animals but for a rainy day outing it passes a couple of hours. Opening hours are Tuesday to Friday from 9am to 7pm and Saturday and Sunday from 10am to 7pm. The adult entry fee is €4 and under 18's and concessions are free.

Villa Durazzo-Pallavicini

Via Ignazio Pallavicini, 13,

16155 Genoa

Tel:+39 010 6672269

www.villapallavicini.info/

This pretty villa sits in a notable 19th century park in one of the suburbs of Genoa and houses the Ligurian Archeological Museum. The 97,000m2 botanical garden sprawls across a gentle hillside behind the villa where the garden is arranged as if in some kind of play. The villa is the work of Micele Canzio, a talented painter and decorated who was the set designer at Carlo Felice, a famous theatre in Italy. His love of the theatre is reflected in the layout of the grounds of Villa Durazzo-Pallavicini.

The park contains numerous statues, ponds, a variety of other structures and an extensive grotto. The grotto is supposed to represent Dantes' Inferno and visitors can descend into the subterranean lake from where they can rise back up again to Paradise.

Visiting Pallavicini will take you on a trip to long ago Liguria when great bears and other now extinct creatures walked the earth. In the Archeological Museum relics of these animals from the Glacial Era, Roman remains and various Paleolithic burials and graves make this an extremely interesting place to visit.

The villa and gardens are open Tuesday to Sunday from 9am all the year round except for over the Christmas period. The Friends of Villa Durazzo Pallavicini organise guided tours of the gardens and all the information is on the website.

Basilica della Santissima Annunziata del Vastato

Piazza della Nunziata

Genoa

Tel: +39 010 2465525

www.annunziatadelvastato.it/

GENOA TRAVEL GUIDE

This is a breathtaking church dating from the 1500's and despite the beauty within it is usually very quiet with few visitors. It is an easy place to visit as it lies between two of the main streets in Genoa, Via Garibaldi and Via Balbi.

From the outside the building is quite plain but inside the frescoes and ornate golden decorations are quite amazing. With light streaming in from both sides the interior is exceptional with a painted and gilded ceiling that appears to be in 3D.

The Basilica is built in a late Gothic style and was dedicated to the patron saint of St. Francis del Guasto. It is seen as one of the churches that displays Genoese art at its best and when you are inside it is easy to see why.

GENOA TRAVEL GUIDE

Lighting a candle when visiting a church is a symbol of an intention to say a prayer for a loved one and the satisfaction of lighting a wax candle can never really be replaced. Basilica della Santissima Annunziata del Vastato in Genoa is one of the few places now where wax candles have not been replaced with the electric variety.

There is a vast amount of art to see in the side chapels and dedicated art lovers might want to visit more than once. Admission is free but contributions are always welcome and you are allowed to a take photos inside. There is a leaflet available in several languages for €1 which explains about the artworks on display.

🌐 Basilica of Santa Maria di Castello

Salita di Santa Maria di Castello 15

Molo, Genoa

Tel: +39 010 2549511

www.santamariadicastello.it/

This religious complex and church can be found in the Castello Hill area of Genoa.

The Romanesque style church was constructed prior to 900AD and houses numerous artworks commissioned by the noblesse of Genoa. Next to the basilica is the impressive Tower of the Embriaci standing at 41 metres high which is the only building in Genoa to have escaped the strict height limits imposed on buildings.

GENOA TRAVEL GUIDE

The Genoan people are very modest and this is shown in the plain exterior of the church that opens up to reveal hidden treasures, gardens and fountains. The frescoes tell the Story of David and the examples from a 16th century Genoan art school of tin-glazed and painted majolicas are quite beautiful. Work can be seen by such illustrious artists are Aurelio Lomi, Giuseppe Palmieri, Lorenzo Fasolo and many others.

There is a volunteer group dedicated to the Basilica Santa Maria di Castello who makes sure that everyone that visits will get the most out of their visit. To help the many tourists they have added 19 information panels and with the help of a local club are translating them into English and other languages.

GENOA TRAVEL GUIDE

The church is open from 10am to 1pm and 3pm to 6pm Monday to Saturday with a daily service at 6pm. The church is not open at the weekends for visiting but only for the services at 11am and 6pm. Entry is free but donations are welcome to support the work of the volunteers and the upkeep of the church

August is the main holiday time in Genoa when most of the locals go on holiday so you might find that a volunteer is not always on hand to show you hidden secrets and explain the wonderful history of the church.

Budget Tips

🌐 Accommodation

Menta e Basilica, Via Piaggio 10 int. 2, 16136 Genoa

Tel: +39 380 177 5477

www.mentaebasilico.it/

This elegant and romantic guest house can be found in

the Castelletto area of Genoa in an elevated position with splendid views of the town below.

The hosts Francesca, Paola, Carlo speak Italian, English and Spanish and they also have their own wine which is delicious and worth sampling. They will recommend places to eat locally as well as the best attractions to visit.

The rooms are decorated with an Arabians Nights theme with antique furniture, sparkling mirrors, soft lighting and fine linens. A hospitality tray is provided in each room along with fluffy bathrobes in the very modern bathroom.

Breakfast is included in the room price and other facilities at Menta e Basilica are a hot tub and whirlpool for guests to enjoy, Wifi, laundry facilities and a conference room.

Prices per room are between €40 and €80 depending on the time of year.

Genoa Hostel

Via Giovanni Costanzi 120

16135 Genova

Tel. +39 010 2422457

www.ostellogenova.it/

The cheap and cheerful Genoa Hostel is located in a hilly area of this pretty Ligurian city so the views when you get to your accommodation are breathtaking. You can walk to the hostel from the city centre in a few minutes but the walk is quite strenuous due to the location, but there is a scenic bus tour.

There are private rooms with two beds and shared dorms that sleep eight. Some rooms have private bathrooms but the cheapest option is to opt for shared facilities. A bed in a shared dorm costs from €15 sharing a bathroom.

There is free Wifi, free parking, 24 hours reception, a vending machine and areas to sit and chat with other backpackers.

Genoa University

www.universityrooms.com/

This is a great way to find a different place to stay in Genoa. Some of the student accommodation is available all year round and some are only available through the university holidays. Many of the colleges are in parts of

GENOA TRAVEL GUIDE

Genoa that are close to the city centre as well as the Old Port and the seafront.

There are rooms available from as little as €16 per night up to €70 per night in a triple room. You can also purchase a meal voucher for €10 to use in the central dining room. All bed linen and towels are provided, there is a private bathroom and breakfast is included. Wifi is available but there are no televisions in the rooms. The rooms are fairly basic but they have all you need for a good night's sleep.

One of the colleges that guests can stay at is Collegio Emiliani set in a 16th century building in the area of Nervi on the east side of Genoa. There is a library, gardens to relax in, a common room, gym, tennis court, luggage storage, heating and air-conditioning and laundry facilities.

At Collegio Emiliani there is a small shared kitchen for guests to prepare snacks as well as bar in the courtyard and several vending machines.

Mini Hotel

Via Lomellini 6/1, 16124 Genoa

Tel: +39 010 2465803

www.minihotelgenova.com/

This hotel has great access to all the attractions in Genoa, the Genoa Principe train station is 200 metres away and a five minute walk takes you to the Old Port and the aquarium. It is located in front of one of Italy's museums from the unification period, in this case the house of Italian patriot and activist Giuseppe Mazzini.

The Mini Hotel offers fast check-in /check-out, luggage storage and a wake-up service. There is a vending machine for drinks, a laundry service and Italian, French and English are spoken.

A single room can be booked from €39; this includes breakfast, free Wifi, air-conditioning, flat-screen TV and a private bathroom. There are 15 rooms and twin bedded and family rooms are available.

Morali Palace Guest House

Piazza della Raibetta 2/28, Genoa

Tel: +39 010 089 9269

www.palazzomorali.com/

GENOA TRAVEL GUIDE

This small and cosy guest house is near the Old Port in Genoa. Housed in a charming 18th century townhouse the Morali Palace Guest House is close to all the main attractions of the town and for travelling further afield the taxi, metro and bus stops are just outside.

Guests can wander under the porches of Sottoripa or explore the hundreds of coffee shops, restaurants and boutiques all a short stroll away.

A double room with a private bathroom is €85 and triple bedded and four bedded rooms are available. All the rooms are comfortably furnished in and an elegant and refined style and offer views across the cathedral or the nearby aquarium. Parking is available nearby at €15 per day and it is sensible to book in advance.

🌐 Restaurants, Cafés & Bars

Gio Pizza

Via M. Novaro 47-49r

16143 Genoa

Tel: +39 010 5298481

www.giopizzagenova.it/

This super friendly pizzeria is just round the corner from the Porta Soprana and is very, very popular. This is a place usually only used by locals and from the prices and pizzas you can see why they want to keep it a secret.

The pizzas are all freshly made and topped with locally grown ingredients. You can choose from the plain margherita to pizzas covered with gorgonzola, salami, mushrooms or lots of other exciting ingredients. There is also a selection of farinata, focaccia, soft drinks and beers.

Gio Pizza is open every day from 5.30pm until 10.30pm and lunchtimes from Tuesday to Friday from 12.30pm to 2.30pm.

Pastaway

Via San Vincenzo, 51r

16121 Genoa

Tel: +39 010 562860

Pastaway is self-service and fast food Italian style. The handmade fresh pasta is served quickly and on a ready to go basis accompanied by a selection of sauces.

You can never go wrong with a box of delicious trofie, a short and twisted pasta, mixed in with pesto for €4-€7. If you don't fancy pesto choose from pomodoro, or walnut or any of the other great flavours on offer. Not just pasta but you can also have rice or ravioli with your chosen sauce.

Open all day until late in the evening Pastaway also has a sit-down area where you can enjoy beer and wine with your pasta.

Bar Tavola Calda Mamacla

P. Colombo

16121 Genoa

Tel: + 342 0355456

Mamacla is a snack bar right in the heart of Genoa where

diners can enjoy traditional Ligurian specialties. They are open all day so whether you are looking for breakfast, lunch or dinner you are sure to find something on the menu to your taste.

High on a Ligurian menu is always focaccia, the unleavened flatbread best eaten warm from the oven. Pesto is everywhere as the main ingredients of pine nuts and basil are grown in profusion locally.

The local pastas on offer of fidellini and trenette are delicious and make a change from the more usual spaghetti and macaroni that most people are used to.

Storico Lounge Café

Piazza de Ferrari Raffaele

16121 Genova

GENOA TRAVEL GUIDE

Tel: +39 010 247 4548

This is a café with a difference. The drinks are all at one price which makes it expensive if you only want a glass of wine. The plus side is that when you have bought your drink you can choose all you can eat from the buffet of salads, meat, BBQ, vegetables and fried food.

The wine selection is varied and the helpful staff will help diners choose which one is best for them. It is in the centre of Genoa and the prices reflect this but you do get great views of the Opera House. Storico does get very busy but then you get the real feeling of a buzzing Italian city which is all part of the experience.

Antica Sciamadda

Via San Giorgio 14

Genoa

Tel: + 39 010 2468516

Farinata shops have been subject to much resurrection lately in Genoa and this one is no exception. Antica Sciamadda is close to the aquarium and the historical town centre and is run by friendly Italians slaving away over their hot ovens.

This tiny little pink fronted shop doesn't look much from the outside but if you watch the steady stream of clientele you know something must be good.

The farinata is simple to make from chickpea flour, water and olive oil and is eaten warm with salt and pepper. Similar to a griddle cake or pancake it is made in huge rounds and cut into individual slices.

Some farinata have onions in but the one of the most famous is the farinata with whitebait. If you are not a chickpea fan Antica Sciamadda also sells various types of focaccia, vegetable tarts and other items.

🌐 Shopping

Mercato Orientale

Via XX Settembre, 272,

Genoa

www.mercatoorientale.org/

It might seem that the Genoan people are doing their

utmost to keep the Mercato Orientale a secret as there are hardly any signs to follow and no grand market entrance. Find your way to XX Settembre and the church of La Consolazione and follow the locals through a passageway and you will come out by the fruit and flower stalls. You can also access the market from the alleys of Via Galata and Piazza Colombo.

This is a market with two levels and on the ground floor the brightest coloured and best foods are artfully arranged to catch the eye of the Italian housewife, and everyone else of course. The produce changes very much with the seasons and the array of food available is quite startling.

Locally grown in Prà the fresh and fragrant basil is top of the list for many shoppers, ready to chop up and add to plump tomatoes, garlic and some delicious local olive oil.

There is fresh fish from the Gulf of Genoa as well as the French coast and in the autumn months chestnuts and mushrooms appear, picked from the local mountains.

There is a superb selection of dried, pickled, bottled and preserved goods available year round plus hams, cheeses, poultry and other delicacies.

The Mercato Orientale is open every day except for Sunday. Trading hours are 7.30am to 1pm and 3.30pm to 7.30pm.

Centro Commerciale Fiumara

Via Fiumara, 15/16

16149 Genoa

Tel: +39 010 460976

www.fiumara.net/

For shopping all under one roof Fiumara is Genoa's biggest shopping centre and is located in the area of Sampierdarena. Free car parking makes going here much easier than visiting some of the smaller shops and with around 85 stores plus bars, restaurants and cinema there is enough to keep you entertained all day.

The centre is open every day from noon until 2am and until 4am on Friday and Saturday.

Via Soziglia

Old Town Genoa

This is the heart of the medieval shopping centre in Genoa and it is where the smaller speciality and gift shops can be found. Generally the opening hours of the shops are 9am to 1pm and then from around 4pm to maybe 7pm or an hour later in summer.

If you are heading into town from the port walk up Via Degli Orefici which lead you into Via Soziglia. If you are feeling in need of refreshments before you browse round the shops try one of the apple strudels at the pastry shop or for a savoury choice there is an excellent focaccia shop.

Traditional gifts and souvenirs to be found in this Ligurian region are beautiful filigree silver and gold jewellery, hand carved wooden objects and handmade lace. For foodie types the delicious and luxurious chocolates are a must and everyone should buy at least one jar of locally made pesto.

There are also fruit shops, shops that sell the dried, salted cod called stoccafish and butcher's amongst the quaint little shops that line this atmospheric and very definitely Italian street.

Guarnimobili

Via di San Lorenzo, 9

16123 Genoa

Tel: +39 010 2468945

It might seem rather strange to visit a shop that sells buttons and door handles when you are on holiday but Guarnimobili is a rather unusual kind of shop. For more than half a century the Genoan people have been able to come here and buy delicately crafted and individual buckles, bells and other metal items.

If you fancy choosing some buttons to brighten up your clothes while you are in Genoa you will be please to find that the shop also sells needles, thread and thimbles. There are over 15,000 items to choose from so a visit could take a while.

Francesco Guarino

Corso Mazzini N.46, Albisola Superiore 17011 Savona

Tel: +39 019 400 4003

www.ceramicheguarino.com/

Take a few hours off from Genoa and head off to the pretty area of Albisola Marina about 35 km's away. Enjoy a gentle stroll along the Artists' promenade and admire the beautiful works of art in mosaic form. Inaugurated in 1963 the walk is considered unique in Europe and dedicated to the artists who have lived and worked in the town.

Albisola pottery is easily recognisable by its traditional blue and white colours. Many of the scenes are biblical with mythological landscapes, cherubs and plants swirling around on a cloudy background. It is pleasing to see that the craftsmen, and women, in the town are working hard at handing on centuries old traditions to the younger generations.

A few streets behind the promenade in Albisola Superiore is the shop of Francesco Guarino where pieces of this beautiful pottery can be bought as reminders of a wonderful holiday on the Italian Riviera.

GENOA TRAVEL GUIDE

The shop is open Monday to Saturday from 8am to 12.30pm and 2.30pm to 7.30pm.

Know Before You Go

 Entry Requirements

By virtue of the Schengen agreement, travellers from other countries in the European Union do not need a visa when visiting Italy. Additionally Swiss travellers are also exempt. Visitors from certain other countries such as the USA, Canada, Japan, Israel, Australia and New Zealand do not need visas if their stay in Italy does not exceed 90 days. When entering Italy you will be required to make a declaration of presence, either at the airport, or at a police station within eight days of arrival. This applies to visitors from other Schengen countries, as well as those visiting from non-Schengen countries.

Health Insurance

Citizens of other EU countries are covered for emergency health care in Italy. UK residents, as well as visitors from Switzerland are covered by the European Health Insurance Card

(EHIC), which can be applied for free of charge. Visitors from non-Schengen countries will need to show proof of private health insurance that is valid for the duration of their stay in Italy (that offers at least €37,500 coverage), as part of their visa application. No special vaccinations are required.

🌍 Travelling with Pets

Italy participates in the Pet Travel Scheme (PETS) which allows UK residents to travel with their pets without requiring quarantine upon re-entry. Certain conditions will need to be met. The animal will have to be microchipped and up to date on rabies vaccinations. In the case of dogs, a vaccination against canine distemper is also required by the Italian authorities. When travelling from the USA, your pet will need to be micro-chipped or marked with an identifying tattoo and up to date on rabies vaccinations. An EU Annex IV Veterinary Certificate for Italy will need to be issued by an accredited veterinarian. On arrival in Italy, you can apply for an EU pet passport to ease your travel in other EU countries.

🌍 Airports

Fiumicino – Leonardo da Vinci International Airport (FCO) is one of the busiest airports in Europe and the main international airport of Italy. It is located about 35km southwest of the historical quarter of Rome. Terminal 5 is used for trans-Atlantic and international flights, while Terminals 1, 2 and 3 serve mainly for domestic flights and medium haul flights to other European destinations. Before Leonardo da Vinci replaced it, the **Ciampino–G. B. Pastine International Airport** (CIA) was the main international airport servicing Rome and Italy. It is one of the oldest airports in the country still in use. Although it declined in importance, budget airlines such as Ryanair boosted its air traffic in recent years. The airport is used by Wizz Air, V Bird, Helvetic, Transavia Airlines, Sterling, Ryanair, Thomsonfly, EasyJet, Air Berlin, Hapag-Lloyd Express and Carpatair.

Milan Malpensa Airport (MXP) is the largest of the three airports serving the city of Milan. Located about 40km northwest of Milan's city center, it connects travellers to the regions of Lombardy, Piedmont and Liguria. **Milan Linate Airport** (LIN) is Milan's second international airport. **Venice Marco Polo Airport** (VCE) provides access to the charms of Venice. **Olbia Costa Smeralda Airport** (OLB) is located near Olbia, Sardinia. Main regional airports are **Guglielmo Marconi Airport** (BLQ), an international airport servicing the region of Bologna, **Capodichino Airport** at Naples (NAP), **Pisa International Airport** (PSA), formerly Galileo Galilei Airport, the main airport serving Tuscany, **Sandro Pertini Airport** near Turin (TRN), **Cristoforo Colombo** in Genoa (GOA), **Punta**

Raisi Airport in Palermo (PMO), **Vincenzo Bellini Airport** in Catania (CTA) and **Palese Airport** in Bari (BRI).

🌍 Airlines

Alitalia is the flag carrier and national airline of Italy. It has a subsidiary, Alitalia CityLiner, which operates short-haul regional flights. Air Dolomiti is a regional Italian based subsidiary of of the Lufthansa Group. Meridiana is a privately owned airline based at Olbia in Sardinia.

Fiumicino - Leonardo da Vinci International Airport serves as the main hub for Alitalia, which has secondary hubs at Milan Linate and Milan Malpensa Airport. Alitalia CityLiner uses Fiumicino – Leonardo da Vinci International Airport as main hub and has secondary hubs at Milan-Linate, Naples and Trieste. Fiumicino – Leonardo da Vinci International Airport is also one of two primary hubs used by the budget Spanish airline Vueling. Milan Malpensa Airport is one of the largest bases for the British budget airline EasyJet. Venice Airport serves as an Italian base for the Spanish budget airline, Volotea, which provides connections mainly to other destinations in Europe. Olbia Costa Smeralda Airport (OLB), located near Olbia, Sardinia is the primary base of Meridiana, a private Italian Airline in partnership with Air Italia and Fly Egypt.

🌍 Currency

Italy's currency is the Euro. It is issued in notes in denominations of €500, €200, €100, €50, €20, €10 and €5. Coins are issued in denominations of €2, €1, 50c, 20c, 10c, 5c, 2c and 1c.

🌍 Banking & ATMs

Using ATMs or Bancomats, as they are known in Italy, to withdraw money is simple if your ATM card is compatible with the MasterCard/Cirrus or Visa/Plus networks. There is a €250 limit on daily withdrawals. Italian machines are configured for 4-digit PIN numbers, although some machines will be able to handle longer PIN numbers. Bear in mind some Bancomats can run out of cash over weekends and that the more remote villages may not have adequate banking facilities so plan ahead.

🌍 Credit Cards

Credit cards are valid tender in most Italian businesses. While Visa and MasterCard are accepted universally, most tourist oriented businesses also accept American Express and Diners Club. Credit cards issued in Europe are smart cards that that are fitted with a microchip and require a PIN for each transaction. This means that a few ticket machines, self-service vendors and other businesses may not be configured to accept the older magnetic strip credit cards. Do remember to advise your bank or credit card company of your travel plans before leaving.

🌐 Tourist Taxes

Tourist tax varies from city to city, as each municipality sets its own rate. The money is collected by your accommodation and depends on the standard of accommodation. A five star establishment will levy a higher amount than a four star or three star establishment. You can expect to pay somewhere between €1 and €7 per night, with popular destinations like Rome, Venice, Milan and Florence charging a higher overall rate. In some regions, the rate is also adjusted seasonally. Children are usually exempt until at least the age of 10 and sometimes up to the age of 18. In certain areas, disabled persons and their companions also qualify for discounted rates. Tourist tax is payable directly to the hotel or guesthouse before the end of your stay.

🌐 Reclaiming VAT

If you are not from the European Union, you can claim back VAT (Value Added Tax) paid on your purchases in Italy. The VAT rate in Italy is 21 percent and this can be claimed back on your purchases if certain conditions are met. The merchant needs to be partnered with a VAT refund program. This will be indicated if the shop displays a "Tax Free" sign. The shop assistant will fill out a form for reclaiming VAT. When you submit this at the airport, you will receive your refund.

🌍 Tipping Policy

If your bill includes the phrase "coperto e servizio", that means that a service charge or tip is already included. Most waiting staff in Italy are salaried workers, but if the service is excellent, a few euros extra would be appreciated.

🌍 Mobile Phones

Most EU countries, including Italy use the GSM mobile service. This means that most UK phones and some US and Canadian phones and mobile devices will work in Italy. While you could check with your service provider about coverage before you leave, using your own service in roaming mode will involve additional costs. The alternative is to purchase an Italian SIM card to use during your stay in Italy.

Italy has four mobile networks. They are TIM, Wind, Vodafone and Tre (3) and they all provide pre-paid services. TIM offers two tourist options, both priced at €20 (+ €10 for the SIM card) with a choice of two packages - 2Gb data, plus 200 minutes call time or internet access only with a data allowance of 5Gb.

Vodafone, Italy's second largest network offers a Vodafone Holiday package including SIM card for €30. They also offer the cheapest roaming rates. Wind offers an Italian Tourist pass for €20 which includes 100 minutes call time and 2Gb data and can be extended with a restart option for an extra €10.

To purchase a local SIM card, you will need to show your passport or some other form of identification and provide your residential details in Italy. By law, SIM registration is required prior to activation. Most Italian SIM cards expire after a 90 day period of inactivity. When dialling internationally, remember to use the (+) sign and the code of the country you are connecting to.

🌍 Dialling Code

The international dialling code for Italy is +39.

🌍 Emergency Numbers

Police: 113

Fire: 115

Ambulance: 118

MasterCard: 800 789 525

Visa: 800 819 014

🌐 Public Holidays

1 January: New Year's Day (Capodanno)

6 January: Day of the Epiphany (Epifania)

March-April: Easter Monday (Lunedì dell'Angelo or Pasquetta)

25 April: Liberation Day (Festa della Liberazione)

1 May: International Worker's Day (Festa del Lavoro / Festa dei Lavoratori)

2 June: Republic Day (Festa della Repubblica)

15 August: Assumption Day (Ferragosto / Assunta)

1 November: All Saints Day (Tutti i santi / Ognissanti)

8 December: Immaculate Conception (Immacolata Concezione / Immacolata)

25 December: Christmas Day (Natale)

26 December: St Stephen's Day (Santo Stefano)

A number of Saints days are observed regionally throughout the year.

🌐 Time Zone

Italy falls in the Central European Time Zone. This can be calculated as Greenwich Mean Time/Coordinated Universal Time (GMT/UTC) +2; Eastern Standard Time (North America) -6; Pacific Standard Time (North America) -9.

🌐 Daylight Savings Time

Clocks are set forward one hour on 29 March and set back one hour on 25 October for Daylight Savings Time.

🌐 School Holidays

The academic year begins in mid September and ends in mid June. The summer holiday is from mid June to mid September, although the exact times may vary according to region. There are short breaks around Christmas and New Year and also during Easter. Some regions such as Venice and Trentino have an additional break during February for the carnival season.

🌐 Trading Hours

Trading hours for the majority of shops are from 9am to 12.30pm and then again from 3.30pm to 7.30pm, although in some areas, the second shift may be from 4pm to 8pm instead. The period between 1pm and 4pm is known in Italy as the *riposo*. Large department shops and malls tend to be open from 9am to 9pm, from Monday to Saturday. Post offices are open from 8.30am to 1.30pm from Monday to Saturday. Most shops and many restaurants are closed on Sundays. Banking hours are from 8.30am to 1.30pm and then again from 3pm to 4pm, Monday to Friday. Most restaurants are open from noon till

2.30pm and then again from 7pm till 11pm or midnight, depending on the establishment. Nightclubs open around 10pm, but only liven up after midnight. Closing times vary, but will generally be between 2am and 4am. Museum hours vary, although major sights tend to be open continuously and often up to 7.30pm. Many museums are closed on Mondays.

🌐 Driving Laws

The Italians drive on the right hand side of the road. A driver's licence from any of the European Union member countries is valid in Italy. Visitors from non-EU countries will require an International Driving Permit that must remain current throughout the duration of their stay in Italy.

The speed limit on Italy's autostrade is 130km per hour and 110km per hour on main extra-urban roads, but this is reduced by 20km to 110km and 90km respectively in rainy weather. On secondary extra-urban roads, the speed limit is 90km per hour; on urban highways, it is 70km per hour and on urban roads, the speed limit is 50km per hour. You are not allowed to drive in the ZTL or Limited Traffic Zone (or *zona traffico limitato* in Italian) unless you have a special permit.

Visitors to Italy are allowed to drive their own non-Italian vehicles in the country for a period of up to six months. After this, they will be required to obtain Italian registration with Italian licence plates. Italy has very strict laws against driving under the influence of alcohol. The blood alcohol limit is 0.05 and drivers caught above the limit face penalties such as fines of up to €6000, confiscation of their vehicles, suspension of their licenses and imprisonment of up to 6 months. Breathalyzer tests are routine at accident scenes.

🌐 Drinking Laws

The legal drinking age in Italy is 16. While drinking in public spaces is allowed, public drunkenness is not tolerated. Alcohol is sold in bars, wine shops, liquor stores and grocery shops.

🌐 Smoking Laws

In 2005, Italy implemented a policy banning smoking from public places such as bars, restaurants, nightclubs and working places, limiting it to specially designated smoking rooms. Further legislation banning smoking from parks, beaches and stadiums is being explored.

🌐 Electricity

Electricity: 220 volts

Frequency: 50 Hz

Italian electricity sockets are compatible with the Type L plugs, a plug that features three round pins or prongs, arranged in a straight line. An alternate is the two-pronged Type C Euro adaptor. If travelling from the USA, you will need a power converter or transformer to convert the voltage from 220 to 110, to avoid damage to your appliances. The latest models of many laptops, camcorders, mobile phones and digital cameras are dual-voltage with a built in converter.

🌐 Tourist Information (TI)

There are tourist information (TI) desks at each of the terminals of the Leonardo da Vinci International Airport, as well as interactive Information kiosks with the latest touch-screen technology. In Rome, the tourist office can be found at 5 Via Parigi, near the Termini Station and it is identified as APT, which stands for Azienda provinciale del Turismo. Free maps and brochures of current events are available from tourist kiosks.

Several of the more tourist-oriented regions of Italy offer tourist cards that include admission to most of the city's attractions. While these cards are not free, some offer great value for money. A variety of tourism apps are also available online.

🌐 Food & Drink

Pasta is a central element of many typically Italian dishes, but there are regional varieties and different types of pasta are matched to different sauces. Well known pasta dishes such as lasagne and bolognaise originated in Bologna. Stuffed pasta is popular in the northern part of Italy, while the abundance of seafood and olives influences southern Italian cuisine. As far as pizza goes, the Italians differentiate between the thicker Neapolitan pizza and the thin crust Roman pizza, as well as white pizza, also known as focaccia and tomato based pizza. Other standards include minestrone soup, risotto, polenta and a variety of cheeses, hams, sausages and salamis. If you are on a budget, consider snacking on stuzzichini with a few drinks during happy hour which is often between 7 and 9pm. The fare can include salami, cheeses, cured meat, mini pizzas, bread, vegetables, pastries or pate. In Italy, Parmesan refers only to cheese originating from the area surrounding Parma. Favorites desserts include tiramisu or Italian gelato.

Italians enjoy relaxing to aperitifs before they settle down to a meal and their favorites are Campari, Aperol or Negroni, the famous Italian cocktail. Wine is enjoyed with dinner. Italy is particularly famous for its red wines. The best known wine regions are Piedmont, which produces robust and dry reds, Tuscany and Alto Adige, where Alpine soil adds a distinctive acidity. After the meal, they settle down to a glass of limoncello, the country's most popular liqueur, or grappa, which is distilled from grape seeds and stems, as digestive. Other options in this class include a nut liqueur, nocino, strawberry based Fragolino Veneto or herbal digestives like gineprino, laurino or mirto. Italians are also fond of coffee. Espresso is drunk through throughout the day, but cappuccino is considered a morning drink. The most popular beers in Italy are Peroni and Moretti.

 Websites

http://vistoperitalia.esteri.it/home/en

This is the website of the Consulate General of Italy. Here you can look up whether you will need a visa and also process your application online.

http://www.italia.it/en/home.html

The official website of Italian tourism

http://www.italia.it/en/useful-info/mobile-apps.html

Select the region of your choice to download a useful mobile app to your phone.

http://www.italylogue.com/tourism

http://italiantourism.com/index.html

http://www.reidsitaly.com/

http://wikitravel.org/en/Italy

https://www.summerinitaly.com/

http://www.accessibleitalianholiday.com/

Planning Italian vacations around the needs of disabled tourists.